Character Education

Cooperation

by Lucia Raatma

Consultant:
Madonna Murphy, Ph.D.
Associate Professor of Education
University of St. Francis, Joliet, Illinois
Author, *Character Education in America's
Blue Ribbon Schools*

Bridgestone Books
an imprint of Capstone Press
Mankato, Minnesota

Bridgestone Books are published by Capstone Press
151 Good Counsel Drive, P.O. Box 669, Mankato, Minnesota 56002
http://www.capstone-press.com

Library of Congress Cataloging-in-Publication Data
Raatma, Lucia.
  Cooperation/by Lucia Raatma.
    p. cm.—(Character education)
  Includes bibliographical references and index.
  Summary: Explains the virtue of cooperation and how readers can practice it at
home, in the community, and with each other.
    ISBN 0-7368-0506-0
    1. Cooperativeness—Moral and ethical aspects—Juvenile literature.
[1. Cooperativeness.] I. Title. II. Series.
BJ1533.C74 R23 2000
179'.9—dc21   99-047924

Editorial Credits
Karen L. Daas, editor; Steve Christensen, cover designer; Kimberly Danger,
  photo researcher

Photo Credits
Corbis, 18
International Stock/Vessey and Vanderberg, cover
Paul McMahon, 16
Photo Network/Myrleen Cate, 4, 8, 20; Jeffry W. Myers, 14
Richard B. Levine, 10
Uniphoto, 6; Uniphoto/Dany Krist, 12

1 2 3 4 5 6 05 04 03 02 01 00

Table of Contents

Cooperation

Cooperation means working with others on a common task. Cooperative people work together to reach goals. Big tasks seem smaller when each person does one part of the task. A group often can reach a goal that one person cannot.

goal
something that you plan
for or work toward finishing

Being Cooperative

Cooperative people help each other complete tasks. You may want to build a treehouse. But you cannot hold a board and pound a nail at the same time. You can cooperate with a friend. Your friend can hold the board while you pound the nail.

Cooperation with Your Family

You may not want to do what your parents ask of you. But they need your help to complete household tasks. You can share chores with a brother or a sister. You can cooperate by setting the table together.

Cooperation with Your Friends

Cooperating with your friends means making compromises. You may want to ride bikes. Your friend may want to jump rope. You can cooperate by taking turns with one another. You can do different activities together on different days.

compromise

to agree to something that
is not exactly what you want

Cooperation in Sports

Cooperating in sports is about playing as a team. One person cannot score points in a football game without help from other players. Teammates cooperate with one another by working together. The whole team helps win the game.

Cooperation at School

Getting along with others is an important part of school. You can cooperate at school by doing what your teachers ask of you. Cooperative students share responsibility for group projects. Everyone needs to work together to finish the project.

responsibility

a task you must complete; each person usually has responsibility for one part of a group project.

Cooperation in Your Community

A community needs the cooperation of the people who live there. People cooperate by helping one another. You can help your neighbors clean up their yards. You can cooperate with others to make your neighborhood beautiful.

"From the time we were little children, my brother and myself lived together, played together, worked together, and, in fact, thought together."
—Wilbur Wright

The Wright Brothers' Cooperation

Wilbur and Orville Wright were brothers. They worked together to invent the first airplane. Wilbur and Orville shared ideas about how to make a plane fly. In 1903, the Wright Brothers made the first flight at Kill Devil Hills, North Carolina.

Cooperation and You

Cooperating with others is about teamwork. You can become friends with people when you cooperate. You rely on others. They rely on you too. Cooperation teaches you to work together with others.

Hands On: Community Cleanup

A job sometimes can seem very big. But the job can be much easier when people work together. Cleaning up a local park builds cooperation in your community.

What You Need
Rakes
Garbage bags
Work gloves
Neighbors

What You Do
1. Pick a local park that needs to be cleaned.
2. Ask your neighbors to come to the park.
3. Clean the park. Some people can rake. Other people can pick up trash and place the trash in garbage bags.

You and your team will feel good as you work together to clean the park. The job gets done faster when everyone cooperates. You can enjoy playing together in a clean park.

Words to Know

compromise (KOM-pruh-mize)—to agree to something that is not exactly what you want

goal (GOHL)—something that you plan for or work toward finishing

rely (ri-LYE)—to trust in or depend on something or someone

responsibility (ri-spon-suh-BIL-uh-tee)—a task you must complete; each person usually has responsibility for one part of a group project.

success (suhk-SESS)—a good outcome or the results that were hoped for

Read More

Hallinan, P. K. *Let's Play as a Team.* Nashville, Tenn.: Ideals Children's Books, 1996.

Hudson, Margaret. *The Wright Brothers.* Lives and Times. Des Plaines, Ill.: Heinemann Interactive Library, 1999.

Joseph, Paul. *The Wright Brothers.* Inventors. Minneapolis: Abdo & Daughters, 1996.

Internet Sites

Adventures from the Book of Virtues Home Page
http://www.pbs.org/adventures
Character Counts! National Home Page
http://www.charactercounts.org
Wright Brothers National Memorial
http://www.nps.gov/wrbr/wright.htm

Index